IN THE CITY OF GLIMMER AND ACHE

coppery green lichens
traces of rose in the stones
a pathway in sunlight
like everything else
obvious, hidden

IN THE CITY OF GLIMMER AND ACHE

Poems by Chuck Tripi

Cyberwit.net
HIG 45 Kaushambi Kunj, Kalindipuram
Allahabad - 211011 (U.P.) India
http://www.cyberwit.net
Tel: +(91) 9415091004
E-mail: info@cyberwit.net

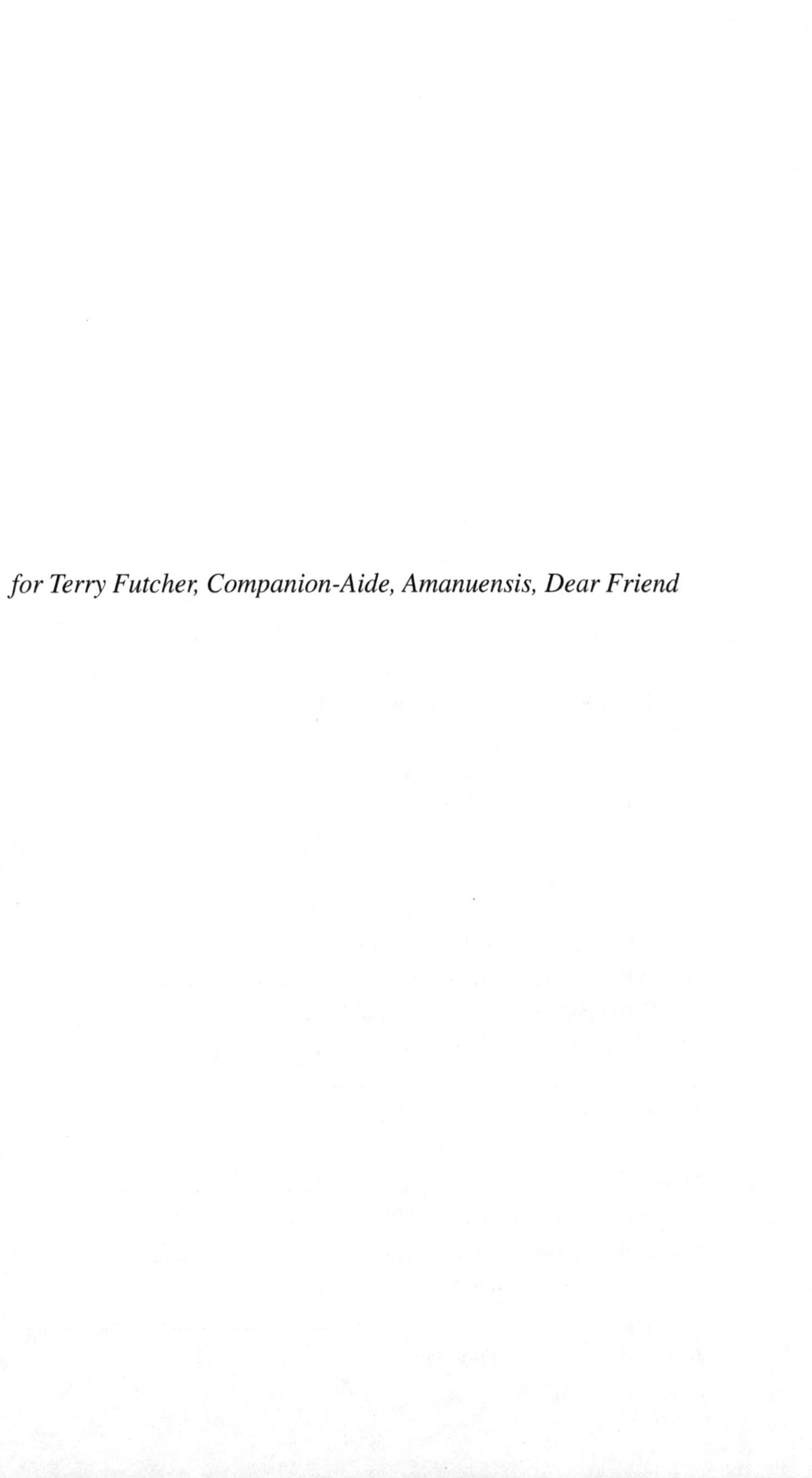

for Terry Futcher, Companion-Aide, Amanuensis, Dear Friend

Contents

Screen Time

My eyes have been my story, I know
no other. When the leaves come down
in celebrated colors. The hollowed-out
children in the ravaged world. I sit here
somehow thinking it's me. Apart, stuck
in these grooves, I leave the pixels
of my screen to fetch another beer
or maybe a shot. When I was a boy
there was a big, crippled bomber
flying rings around my house, the crew
in calm community, coaxing at the gear.
It finally did come down. Still I see
the glint of sunlight on the fuselage
in pixels too, together, bombs and light.

My Pain Is My Pain

Pain is my companion, ever nearby—
I am the Watcher. I see it arising
from eons ago. The people will say it,
your pain is mine, my pain is for you.
You cannot believe it, this cozy trope—
a wan residuum, this faith left over.

With pain the scintilla of hope will come—
it must. In days of Nero and Caligula
you go for your lunch to the stadium.
You are watching the lions eat men.
Here there are axes and mayhem,
groans in the sun, here is the throng.

Out of disgust and desire comes Providence.
A belly of lunch, lower taxes, just a little bit free
and the people are satisfied, all of the evidence
a rabid, a Roman contrary. My pain is mine.
Your pain is yours. Still, my dear Loves,
when we met at the Circus, you knew me.

In the Silence of Olsen's Pines and Oaks

even the plum blossoms were in another yard
— Basho

All of the lonely sounds are lonelier now
as if music coming from another room
but beautiful. Lilt and light and dark somehow
penetrate into the hurt, into the gloom
as one ineluctable spell and power.
No, they are not really harbingers of doom
although the *caws* from Olsen's pines are near it—
to say the truth, it seems I'll not long hear it.

Nor *susurrus* through his oaks in summertime,
her favorite word and sound and harmony.
Nor his pine boughs cracking under ice, *like chimes,*
she said to me, *the chimes of January.*
No more the whimsy of her Latinate rhymes,
her elegant, deft *hauteur* and mockery
and as the moon-lit pine boughs start to glisten
I will lean toward the trees and hope, and listen.

On the Threshing Floor

Where there is no mill, where there is no creek,
we live at Mill Creek. The Miller seems fled
to his quaint reserve. Cooper and smithy
and wheelwright—we have outlived them
these generations since. Our toiling years,
our time at the anvil or on it have passed
and many an unaccountable thing.
In wonder and mystery trudging these halls
to the mail or a meal, bound, we are free.
Known to one another, our fate is our dignity.
At the end of the path there is bocce,
Monday Memoir, Thursday Philosophy—
current events and a putting green
in seasonal sun and in seasonal rain,
the threshing floor where the Miller sweeps
or plucks us, grain by grain by grain.

As to Our Evening Gaze

We see without seeing, meet without meeting
here at our separate windows each evening
to stare dissolving into our disappearing worlds
in the thousand, the ten thousand stages of grief.

Out there are the fountains, swirling
and spilling away in the cadence of time
in its tyrannical, unfazed continuum.
Elderly walkers in sweaters, deep into August

just such as I. In the courtyards below
not a trace, not a sign of our previous glories,
nothing of stature or status remains—
only our shades at the door, fumbling with our keys.

Westward those undulating, treed hills tend
in seasonal iterations to the Delaware
and maybe halfway there in the Sparta cemetery
with only a single missing date, a stone awaits me.

Dissonance, Retirement Village

I said nothing, complicit and ashamed.
— a resident

We came, so many with our savaged hearts,
our dead in distant, unvisited graves.
Ravages of body and of brain are made
in a merciless progress—inch by inches
go our lives and deaths and desolations.

There is a bar where no one drinks too much
and no one, man or woman seems to flinch
upon our common tragedies, but speaks,
or weeps a little in their turn, full and clear,
an almost loving commonality arisen here

and then with soup and fruit plates, reticence.
Chicken of a dozen different kinds, three of pie
with sugar or without—a mock civility sets in,
eclipsing even just the words—the *words,*
good Christ, *guns* or *lies* or *national disgrace,*

dead children. When the dogwood blossomed
days ago into a puff of cotton candy in the sun,
what I made of it was gunsmoke in our impotent,
murderous land, the crutch of an amendment,
choices we make, the slaughter of the innocent.

Thoughts and Prayers

If it should happen I am blown to bits
at Piggly Wiggly, my tomato bisque
and *Prego* Extra Chunky, salsa dip,
my guts and glands and teeth and shit
and memories all splattered on the cereals,
Cocoa Puffs and Captain Crunch and Cheerios

dear Mayor, keep your prayers to yourself.
This God you made who looks and punishes
and favors, and who thinks the same as you,
who had the time to write the Constitution
cannot hear your feckless twaddle of a prayer
or does not listen or care, or is dead.

At the podium you all appeared again
in the theater of make-believe grief,
tricked-up commiseration and distress
as if it isn't you who makes these laws
you sluts and whores in the spell of donors who,
if really there is a God, will meet you in hell.

Suckers and Losers

> *Into battle, led like cattle*
> *they are heard to sigh,*
> *to the port of embarkations*
> *follow me, and die.*
> — F-105 Alma Mater

Did you take the oath?
Under a thunder of bombers and fighters
the parade grounds shook, and I raised my hand.

Have you attained to valor and glory?
I attained to good fortune and fellowship,
to liar's dice in eight corners of the world,
nosewheel roulette. Taiwan, Turkey, Wake,
Alaska, Berlin. Bragg, Benning. Fort Campbell—
air-dropped the Eighty-Second and the One Hundred-First.
Drank beer with them later in the highest honor of my life,
in their clinic, their shop-talk of glory and valor and death
and found nothing to despise until so much later.

What have you come to despise?
I have known *Wild Weasels* and *River Rats,*
squadrons of men with a loss-rate of half
who grew moustaches, drank rice wine and pressed on
in the fearful nights. Of Thud Ridge and Hanoi,
Voodoo pilots, their job to take pictures in the keen,
lethal sight of the enemy. *Ranch Hand,*
Provider pilots, their fifty-year watch
for a cancerous yield. Our trash-hauling *Hercules.*

An Loc, Kon Tum. Arc Light, Linebacker.
Forgotten names. Those vaults in Arlington.
Normandy, cross by cross by star of American dead
to whom the entire world is forever in debt—
where a man from Queens would withhold his respects,
General Kelly said, so as not to get his hair wet.

Stanzas, from a Patriotic Rage

> *For how can you compete... with one*
> *Who were it proved he lies*
> *Were neither shamed in his own*
> *Nor in his neighbors' eyes?*
>   — William Butler Yeats

In ninety days I took the oath on the parade grounds—
there beneath a thundrous roar still ringing,
every fighter in the inventory, tight formations
wing to wing, the Missing Man, and we were proud,
my late father and I, as he pinned my bars on, bonds
now deeper than our blood, or blood behind or to come
or seas or continents or boundaries forever crossed.

But let there be no stolen valor here—
there was no blood to come for me, and I am glad of it.
I broke those first, leaden wings into halves
in the customary way of courting fate, and after that
our first, our loving frolic of a year
she pinned my father's sterling silver wings on me
and so began my rollicking, undistinguished career.

And now *the days are dragon-ridden* and in Yeats
we see a prophecy where once mere reportage
if captivating and true, of a barbarous age,
and know that we were twitter-pated if we did not see
that prophecy in all the cock-eyed lying oaths, spittle
on the chins of cockamamie congressmen and justices,
a proven liar president who is adored for it.

Here in this pale fire of our flaccid rage,
that longest, inadequate epigraph
with which I cannot compete
an overwhelming fury comes upon me,
images of ill-begotten feathers and horns,
the insincere flag of a fake shaman,
a murderous, gun-drunk citizenry,

the Pimp of Failed Casinos, his insolent fiends,
the nihilists of our trashed American dream
and there is nothing for it,
nothing for the carnage, I mean,
for the amendable amendment, you see,
nothing but to take a knee. Our bitter anthem,
take a knee and Cry, our Beloved Country.

Sorting Mementos, Sunday Afternoon

Wild Weasels, can you believe it,
locked-in, dead center on a radar beam
so to fly right on down it? *Before it gets you,*
you bust it all up into Kingdom-Come,
missile, site, crew, hat, ass and overcoat.
Back at Takhli you drink yourself silly
if only to sleep, if only to dream.
I was no hero, but I knew some.
Huns and *Phantoms, Thud* drivers,
some dead, some alive,
Captain Radcliff, who gave me a check ride
and said *not to worry, Lieutenant, if I am writing—*
it is likely a sonnet for my lovely wife.
He was dead in a year in a place I couldn't pronounce.
He wanted our shoes black, is all—a smooth pitch-out.
A jerk or two, not so many as you might presume.
One little C-7 guy all *to fly and to fight,* his unlikely story—
dropped oil drums on sampans—from Akron Ohio,
who couldn't hit a cow's ass with a banjo.

A couple of very smart guys who knew better,
so smart that they never arrived, so smart
that they died—dead by cleverness.
No, they don't, all of them, become pacifists
and peace is unkind, and war is not glamorous
but for a story embellished by too many drinks, need,
sometimes a desperate, exogenous need
from the past, *not to be wrong—*
not to be wrong in the past, not to be wrong
in the goddamned past.

Same flight suit, same boots, similar patches,
aviator shades and a great big watch,
a cool hat, one saved airplane—ten seconds
out of fifteen thousand hours. A C-130 lapel pin,
no combat time. The sublime and the gruesome
but I guess, yes, we would most of us do it again.
I am no hero, but I knew some.

Having Visions at the Funeral

The buck is back again and still in rut,
stumbling as if drunk into the road.
Tugged by a need, head flung high,
he breathes an evening deep. His throat,
his chest precede him in the rain. Losing
her scent, he snorts at the oncoming cars.

No one comes back. It's the same desire,
only in church this time—the choir sings
May angels welcome you in paradise.
It seems a good idea, a kind of return
if one he cannot reach even in dreams,
though he can hear the angels calling him.

He sits behind the row of widows now
and comes to crave and remember.
A fleshy collage, perfumed
and braceleted, nearly intimate—prayers
for another dead best friend in heaven.
He signs the book, small as a man in love.

Is It Blasphemy

To think you are silent,
silent as the roots,
as bears in winter, nests in rain?
Or is it that the gold and red
flung from the expressive trees in autumn
is a kind of noise?
And the clouds riding stark
through the night before the blinding—
are these the trumpets
of my own migration?
Is it blasphemy
so to see myself amid the evidence
a prime participant,
as if it were I who made it?

Dreaming in Poetry

The Grand Canyon, Northern Lights, Penumbra.
A morning sun on the Cliffs of Dover.
I've seen swans landing on Lake Geneva.
I have read John Keats on Chapman's Homer,
seen the blue of glaciers in Alaska.
I've been around—I know about Wonder.
Be Serene—I tell you with Confidence—
everything Wonderful is Permanent.

These eight lines, then, as to my dear late wife:
since first she studied Virgil's *Aeneid*
she began, and for the rest of her life
without cease in the myriad of nights
whether in a time of ease or of strife
or in an interval of Seneca or of Hesiod
and Wondrous by any parameter—
she dreamed in dactylic hexameter.

I do not come to speak to you of God
in whom I find a doubtful character.
Neither good nor powerful, only odd,
truth be told, no Father, no Arbiter—
most anyone would do a better job.
And still I pray, each night at your picture,
my eternal love, as old people do—
in wonderful Peace, believing in you.

Finger Painting Day in America

— for Finnian

When in hilarious gigantic shirts
and an appropriate solemnity
our little citizens will come to play
in big-shirted ceremony. Of paint,
splatter and story time. In disarray
they have learned to sing together, *Clean-up,*
Clean-up when they've made a mess, keen
to hear the words, *Good job, good job.*
Our fervent mob, grave, good and innocent.
Miss Teacher is getting them civilized,
Mister Comity, Miss Hope and Intent
with their adorable, their bright consent.

On the Immortal Nature of Night Baseball

There was at the bar an old gentleman
alive in Brooklyn Dodger livery
fair to gushing of Reese and Robinson.
'Fifty-five, he says, *still so sweet to me.*
Hodges and Furillo, Duke, Gilliam,
Newk, Drysdale, heaters you can't even see.
And the worst rats ever, if you ask me,
Horace Stoneham and Walter O'Malley.

On this of course, we agree to agree,
remembering the old re-creations.
Huddled with radios under the sheets
for ticker-tape baseball from weak stations,
two little die-hards so soon fast-asleep
in those old, those wonderful frustrations
and it went like this even to last call
as if we were talking about baseball.

As if in that luminous alchemy
in tincture and tincture upon tincture
time has not for us buffered memories
in holy passages, beyond scriptures,
from Adcock, Mathews and Spahn set us free—
Bill Mazeroski, gone from the picture.
There are others more dear in gilded frames—
we speak of them too, so to hear her name.

1970: T-38 Night Solo

My regular instructor is DNIF
so they find me a cadre guy. Wing staff,
you know, desk jock, one step from a RIF,
no real flying job, passed-over twice.
I call Oak City for a torch climb,
light the burners, peg the vvi.
Level at four-one-oh, transonic—
just a flicker on a dial, Mach one,
a little bit more. Ease-off,
check fuel, split S, pop the boards
and dive away home. Ribbon rolls
on downwind he dares me to try,
my landing is crap but he lets me get by.
I know, he says, *your one and only dream—*
I notice you majored in English, though.
So he had done his homework—now I know.
We smoke a few Luckies, he has a beer.
Well, get your 'chute, you better be out of here
and I was going, going and gone,
best time you could have with your clothes on.

Lieutenant Colonel Boyer, You Dick

You see, you teatotaling cracker-ass
telephone colonel, people died from this.
I knew I was right, but not how I felt
there in front of the Squadron Commander
telling you *fly it your effing self, then.*

Thank you for not taking it out on me.
I never heard *boo* so it must have been you
getting those words shoved up your ass—
We want mission hackers here, Lieutenant.
Ass, you, me, cracked valve-housing dangerous

and your silver oak leaves irrelevant.
1972, you never knew,
with three temps maxed, clearing a cliff somewhere
I would not stay in formation with you—
it was my TAC check—he never said *boo.*

I was sitting here thinking of a crew,
crashed on a cliff in '82, of you,
of your ignorant cowboy legacy,
of the endurance of stupidity,
of swagger, leadership, lethality.

An F. N. G. Convinces Me to Quit

I don't like him—we haven't even met.
Gigantic Air Force Academy ring,
calls me *Boss,* wears his hat like a cadet.
A sparrow, I figure he's no eagle. Area qual—
whatever I say he says is illegal.
We're getting off wrong, I'm already raw,
parsing the Air Force, Civil and Moral law.
So he files instruments to Allentown
to a published miss to a published hold
all of which we do, then the freaking clown
with RAPCON watching decides to get bold
and he's fixing to buzz his mother's house
whereupon I take the airplane away,
cancel instruments and turn to the south,
Return To Base, never see this jackass again
nor ever an Air Force installation.

At the Chief Pilot's Office, Checking In

Your hearing improves at the hearing.
              — Tom Pasquale, c. 1961

Good morning Captain, I'm new to the crew base.
This may surprise you: To start with the rules—
these guidelines for the able, wise pilot
require the absolute, the unquestioning
observance of fools. You've heard of dead wrong?
In our ideation, dead right is more likely.

How then is order and discipline maintained?
From consent of the organized comes a safe operation,
from lore, customs and courtesies, sound laws,
paradigm. Universal intolerance of incompetence.
Keen awareness of target fixation
and get-there-itis. Not drinking too much.

Recall the location of your car in the lot,
absorb the ten thousand revisions.
Kiss the dog, pet the spouse on returning home.
If something has gone wrong, protect the crew.
Tell me no lies at the hearing, whatever you do—
I'll do the lying for all of you.

For a Secular Epistemology

Everyman is entitled to his own opinion . . .

They embrace ignorance. What does this mean?
They are preoccupied with *how to do*
who burn the books of how it was *to be.*
They turn the schoolhouse into luxury,
fall in love with proud, big-foot certainties
and stomp like savages on history
with all of its grim inconveniences.

They embrace violence. What does this mean?
They have been seduced by half-sentences
who do not know feeling from opinion,
who from the barstools of America
bray about merit, of *those evil hordes*
colluding ingeniously at the borders
to attain to a breach, to a perfect union.

They reject evidence. What does this mean?
Ah—truth fact reality, opinion,
my truth—but some opinions are bunkum—
this is the second half of the sentence
you loud-mouthed destroyers of common sense,
you feckless vainglorious louts. Poor shards,
poor donkeys. Billygoat Gruffs, you ghost-hearts.

And God is their witness. What does this mean?
They say God is good, God the All-Mighty.

God is dead, they meant. They say that God weeps,
they say Satan comes as a man of peace.
He speaks in self-interest, Everyman,
who cannot know Heaven from Hell.
And if he should learn it, there is no one to tell.

1965: Our Drunken Priest, and Sage

All the world's a bleeping stage, men,
he said, putting to good use
the timeless epithet, *and we*
poor players who but strut and fret—
he lit a cigarette—*our blessed lives*
about upon it, cloaked in tragedy
and ignorance and frailty. For extra credit
promise me you never will forget it—
something like that—words to that effect
for three straight classes once the beer truck
made its monthly visit to the friary.
The Very Reverend Friar Tuck, himself at
the very pinnacle of his career professed
could not have expressed it better than that.
And none would deny but a churlish cur
this merry band of lettered men their beer,
the last honest pleasure left to them here.

How Maddie Makes You Lonesome

There comes with Maddie a brilliant want,
like missing a county in Ireland.
Killarney, Lough Leane, whirlpools of dark,
all of those devils, scaring the children
three-quarters to death.
Bigger kids taunt them at school with it—
an old interference even into dreams,
where soon a Maddie of one's own will appear.
Distant as Lady Gregory, Beatrice riding to hounds,
as here to Sligo. Gnarled, knotted trees by the tower
by the stream, wine with the gods of poetry.
Where famine had scuttled Ireland's hopes—
Black and Tans, a later, a barbarous try.
Two little whiles, this one or that,
those fraught, those ferocious interstices.
But I have had a third tonight
and find myself bitter as to policies here.
Over there, Maddie's kin, their ancient place,
where still they lie in their eternal space,
endlessly wanting their progeny home.

A Know-It-All Walks into a Bar

Maddie don't care for old Doctor Buzz-Crush.
'Talks down to you—and to me in-between—
Limousine Liberal, no limousine.
As for the tips, Maddie says he don't rush.
S'ombitch tells Maddie her mind is all mush,
tells her he writes for a wine magazine,
his thesis on Shaw—*Begin the Beguine.*
Places to be, he says—*sorry to rush.*
Good night Sweetheart. He huffs, *'night gentlemen.*
And we get loud, and we raise up a cheer:
One for all, old Buzz-Crush, have a nice day
we savages say, anarchists, tradesmen,
narcissists bothering Maddie for beer—
All for one—laissez les bons temps rouler.

Log Cabin Nut Brown

Given the way it ends, who knows a heart?
Soul, who knows it, body and mind? Names,
we take the names for it as if we knew,
and squabble at the trickery of names,
the insufficiencies, a heart, a soul, a body,
mind. When Maddie tends the bar the night
comes to, awakens for me into single
perfect moments. Just the right proportions,
Maddie, how she listens to a dolorous
or charming tale. She does not slight the boys,
she does not seem to hear them bragging,
or the belches or their bitches when they
call again, *Maddie, another Nut Brown*!
You know, the ale is perfect. Maddie,
when she draws my glass will make it seem
as if the sun has not and never will go down.

Also at Maddie's Are Friendships Made

You injure me oh brief, taciturn men
who in your time of grief get over it.
Whose turn-taking and topic maintenance,
forlorn as you are, never skip a beat.

Who return to your satisfying work,
dark, stern, grave, a man, presidentially,
watching yourself as if in a mirror
and proud to behold your maturity.

Endomorphs of a bereft New Jersey,
why do you cling to antiquated tropes,
to your disrespectful stiff upper lips—
what's with the insult of your *savoir faire*?

At Maddie's last night, a woman and I,
slightly hammered, simpatico and true
foreswore as one the lugubrious chore
and left—one Uber each, needing no more.

Time to Go

Your stupid generation, my daughters,
not entirely without reason say.
Truly I have seen well-intended friends,
gentlemen of an epic *joie de vivre*
(*Exactly the problem,* those two maintain),
two *different* men and at two different times
in two different *states* vault over the bar,
bow to a pretty barmaid in *gassho* or *namaste*
to a lusty roar and cheers, hers included
though all agreed maybe we should leave now.
Oh taprooms and pals and hilarity,
palm to palm I bow down respectfully.
Making no argument of *time and place,*
context or *era* as anyone might—
a nod and a smile, *namaste,* good night.

A Song for Maddie

There came a time-to-time to Maddie's bar
one of those deluded, ghost-thirsty men
and one of us walked Maddie to her car
so they were mostly never seen again
but to bask sober in her lilt and light,
her unassailable, generous heart.
She had only to glare to stop a fight,
she *knew*. Who was a pair, who was apart.
Our Maddie—bright-smiling, eyes glistening,
and everything just right, or so it seems
here in the bell-beat of remembering.
Whisky or Maddie? Mine or Maddie's dreams—
western shores, of kelp and shells and seafoam,
lowering skies, a song to sing her home.

Of Two Arrows Meeting in the Air

A trope—synchronicity, let's say.
Beyond neural pathways or canonical laws—
a twinge of desire, tinctures of reality.
Tyranny of mind. You say *everything happens
for a reason*. Respectfully I answer,

whatever you mean—*what happens, whatever,*
it's just a result—what happens is caused.
Abundance, a generous universe,
interest, attention to potencies—
all that arises arises from need.

Of superstition and coincidence—
God or not, luck or fate or lottery,
design—two arrows meeting in the air
beyond neural pathways, faith or doubt or not
and each of them caused, and each of them shot.

Thirst

I live in the lighthouse, the way it shines.
Turns of the sea and arcs of the dolphin.
As if those passing boats will ever pass
and keep those buoys *red right returning*.
Workboats, dark smoke, *chuttering*
diesels, lumber and groceries, whisky
on placid or frothy, grayish or green.
I fancy the Captain has quit. Of all manner
of injurious things he has become free
but for the odd flinch or grasping mind.
He finds in the names of things repose—
dory or *skiff, lapped strakes* though his boat,
his boat is no, has no such things. At noon
or a little before, at noon give or take he goes by
on the brightening waters. No hail or salute,
ahoy, no nod even to my service—
as if he will not need my light, and soon.

Dao the New Tao, Chan the Old Zen

There is a dangerous figment afoot
in the notion of this present moment.
There is in the Dao, in the Zen of it
at once, ancestors, legacy, story.
There is no now. We have not understood
who speak of the Dao or Zen of it,
or mean another thing entirely.
No harm has been done, please do not worry—
your shadow covers the ground you walk on.
These unharmable, verymindlike things
go with you in figments or in danger,
a mathematics of Chan, a Dao of Tao
in every imaginable season,
ignorance and misery and delight.

You Will Discover in Delight Again

You will discover again delighted
the joy of your own original mind
where it has lingered long and open-eyed
just for you—your own available mind,
the peerless willing instrument of you.
Orthodoxies fall away. Roshi, rules,
Astral schoolmarms, clucks of knowing tongues,
quibblers as to self and other, dancers
in the moonlight of priests, poets and gods,
priests, poets and gods, faiths of our fathers
if this is the need of your own sweet heart,
boogeyman prophets will all fall away
if you will only wait, our earnest friend,
just exactly there, just exactly there.

This Is How the I Ching Works

It's a little like
What's that guy's name?
Like *Where is my hat* and your hat
just comes flying, right out of the blue.
This is how the I Ching works,
your numbers, your *getting it.*
Something comes up from the deep
with your secrets, sort of calling you.
You may sense a little squeeze
in your hand, like your first- ever movie,
boy-girl. You go someplace after
in a glide, funny and smart, spotlit.
Your secrets are secret from you,
then you know them.

Practicum

Diamond ruby emerald abide in me
in a certain central ground of being,
heat. *Qi*, there is a cold cold clarity.
A part never, a part ever-seeing.
Simple sometimes sometimes complexity,
in a single thing binding and freeing.
Perfect and complete, in pieces undone
I appear in town soul body mind one.

There is a beginning, a destiny
we share, a light to a light to a light
and I am sure dear friend or enemy,
you have seen it too, awakened at night
whether in scarcity or in plenty,
knowing. Nothing to fear. Nothing to fight,
lived the day amnesiac, in tatters.
Please practice this: *Nothing Really Matters.*

Joan and Michael Cannot Know

He called me *silly woman* as he died,
our children, Joan and Michael will attest
and for a year I went to bed and wept
for missing him near me, if not for the rest.
No one manages the losing of a mind,
those creeping, those clouded slippages
into an oblivious cruelty.
Michael says to put it all behind me,
Joan says I take pleasure in these images
cascading down on me, of barrel-houses
and of cigarettes—of driving faster
in the sunset glare and laughter
in our silly mockery of the roads.
And they are right, our Joan and Michael
but to say the truth, some things aside,
what do Joan and Michael know?

Dancing in the Empty Nest

When Michael went away there was a pall,
a mist of silence all come down on us
where once rambunctious pals of his would call—
where *Slayer, Metallica, Incubus.*
Then Joanie leaves, as most of them will do.
Your only daughter, this one hurts the worst.
The meaning of emptiness clear to you
you sit on her bed to cry. Bereft, cursed.
And you have a drink and you pull the drapes
and then another and you lock the door
and care for nothing of your fallen shapes
and toss your clothing on the kitchen floor.
There is nothing to save, nothing to break
and he says *shake it, shake it Baby, shake.*

Chairlift

She arrives at nine to give me my pills,
eyedrops for nighttime and cranberry juice
or a jigger of wine for a rebellious mood.
To get me in bed she says *Now, Missus,*
grunting me up from my chair.
We stow the remote in its proper place,
I like to watch *Morning Joe.* We laugh some
and pray, prayers for dead husbands,
exchange little brags. Our grandsons, *cute
as a button* and *cute as a button,* it seems
they are drifting away. A necessary,
even a good thing, we seem to agree.
I have forgotten, making my nightly mistake—
she says, *no, dear, you've been to Montego Bay.*
Kingston is home to me, Kingston—
Kingston will be my burial place.

To an Old Woman in a Wheelchair

In these the neural pathways of our days
gone by or to come, we dwell wondering
or mindless or indifferent or afraid,
as Buddhas and saints. I look into your eyes
once clouded, maybe, with emergencies or fate
so heavy-lidded now, obsidian or blue,
green along the spectrum of nodding-off.
Some of us court sleep, some awakening,
delicious fictions of a nimble mind
as time, as time will, wears it away.
Yet there in your eyes a glimmering still
of everlasting, final things. Ever true,
a last love, sunset on the placid waters
luminescent, a light, the light in you.

. . . Like an Old Fool

Our children say my love is only loneliness,
just an echo from the chasm of ache.
A howl of an ancient gust come and gone,
the scar of a sweet participation.

Etched, sharp and deep, the letters on our grave
and still the surface is smooth, warm in the sun.
Two stylized angels rise above our names
here where I will join you as dust one day.

And it is true, she talks a little young,
is flighty and *outré,* and *jangles* a bit at dinner.
They are right as to the *daring ensemble,*
and right about this too—*there is no fool . . .*

but they are kind to save me, or to try—
I will have to find a better thing to do
these Sunday afternoons, the haunted hours
weeping in a field of stones and flowers.

Heart Is the Survivor

Heart the survivor inarticulate
from labyrinthine ways returns
quiet and veteran and hidden,
to its very own insights hidden.
When it is broken there is
no plausible chain of denial.
Once mended, last to learn of it,
oblivious Heart, how, a when, a why,
this dumb plodding, this blind Heart,
this absentee from its own affairs,
this unnoticed, this drunken child
at a wedding. Reincarnate
sage of old catastrophe
helpless, *en garde*, recidivist, ready.

Crossing Second Avenue

— for Kieran

Just in case, I tell my grandsons tales
wherein the valorous reap glory.
On the matter of risk I offer pause,
as to a gory death, I say nothing
even as fear, as each crossing haunts me—
bike paths, buses, madmen, delivery vans,
honk and blare, a lethal river, this side
or that, the odd splatter of boy or man.
The oldest does not see it, exactly,
but yearns in the old way for the big idea.
Exalted at the crossing, close to home
he will take my dangling, useless hand
when I forget to offer it—he reaches
for me, knowing soon as children do
that I am dreaming. Of an irresponsibility,
of a burgeoning freedom. Actuarial tables,
a macabre beauty, of a sweet impossibility.

Note to My Grandsons

The People say it is temporary
though *affaires de coeur* will make evident,
poor playthings, all of it is permanent.
There is little beneath you or above
your stalwart aching brazen helpless heart—
who is not a fool has not been in love.
Love is the stalker. Guile or pretense, art,
swift feet, training get no one free of it.
Earnest sincerity, truth, falsity,
there is no respite—there is no exit
to a last breath—even, I think, in death.
Order, chaos, agony and delight,
but love. Love. Love with flare and grace and might
and never play love, and never play fight.

In the City of Glimmer and Ache

— for Cavan

Ache, and *wonder,* these are my go-to words,
arising in most every utterance.
An almost iambics, *beyondishness,*
the hurt of belonging, at a distance.

And Cavan has joined the poetry club.
Middle-guy-serious, the sensitive one,
he will burst with the ten thousand questions,
the ache and the wonder of poems in the city.

Of the potted gingko, what is nature,
in all of this brick and cement, what is not,
the taxis and stoplights, a *chuttering* bus—
street drugs, of guns, of legendary crime?

What to say of the old suburbanite
still holding sway over our poetry,
an eclipsed, centenarian legacy—
there are, dear Cavan, ideas beyond things.

Beyond potted gingkoes, floral hues
along Park Avenue, want, noise and glimmer,
a rheumy-eyed grate-sleeper, glaring at you—
this is your home, where everything is two.

First Comes Desire

Of Origins, Great Matters, The Big Want.
We sit down to it, my grandson and I
at dinner in his favorite restaurant.
Two steaks, a Shirley Temple and red wine
and bread and olive oil and argument.
Proof by Design is all I remember—
we are doubters each of us, in shadows,
it seems impossible really to *know.*

Walking home together I am teetering
in shame and reproach—what have I taken
from this ten-year-old boy—I speak too freely.
What wonder and delight, what hope and ache,
what bond and vision, word, rite and teaching
and beyond all this, who am I to say?
Each affirmation hides its opposite—
consciousness is conflict: *There is a God,*
 a good God who loves you I almost scream
as we are crossing Second Avenue.

Just yesterday too, I swirled gelato
into strawberry soup, tasted complexity
and named it wonderful. I have not seen
beyond a glimmer nor heard beyond noise
though I name it good, and hope it is so.
Maybe he will hear and see one day
set free in the Great Conclusion too—
of what is good, or beautiful or true,
first comes desire, then belief, then proof.

Melodiam Desiderata

> *Woman is fickle and changeable.*
> — Virgil in *The Aeneid*

It means *the song I want to hear,* maybe.
You said *Femina varium et mutabile semper.*
I heard in it your arch mockery—I had no Virgil,
used a pony for Ovid and Catullus, failed Tacitus.

As *Angelus* rang through the valley though,
upon the hilltop of our generations, we sang too
if only for that while. And when you walked out
on the brimstone of that silly Bishop I was proud.

For fifty years then *blessed angels sang* to you
above the Babel sounds their canonical hours,
Magnificat, Magnificat and *Alleluia,* Faith
and Hope and Love and Providence and still

I only sometimes hear them. Now and then
at night before your picture, praying to a God
I do not know I hear your mocking dactyls, see
your arching brow and believe we will meet again.

Like Rain in December

We know who we are, men with dead wives.
Wives in memory care. Wives in hospice.
A stoic fraternity of little hope,
an unfamiliar quietude.

Oh maybe with whisky, at dinner
we say lonesome, beautiful things
or lonesome, wistful things
but little. Of what is most terribly missed—
It's all for the best, we say, *it is what it is.*

It wasn't supposed to be this way—
this unimagined longevity.
These wrong, asymmetrical endings—
we were to be gone. *We* were to be spent.

Another whisky, then, no more.
It is like rain in December, so:
clutching our collars,
hunched against weather,
hastening home.

To Sit Here at Night Alone

In the embrace of time, turning to you
still, seems a proof and verification.
Things left to say, things left to talk about
prove in a generous way there is time.
This is to be a part, to be apart,
we were not first to die or die nearly
if one of us late, one of us early
an urge and flinch, a something to tell you—
I have seen it, the river of time too
but find no practical application.
A continuous continuum, good,
true and spare. Like a heartbeat still going on—
a body and mind entirely of air
you are gone, my Love, eternally there.

Into a Moonless Black

Theodore Roethke's "Night Crow," for instance
seems a perfect depiction of the word
vastation. It isn't used anymore
lacking as it does the density of, say
the anthracite heart of a beaten child
later, the shock and the hurt gone away
to a heatless, obsidian self-blame.
Afflicted, adrift, a betrayed innocent
and lucky for you if it makes no sense,
the next-day embrace of the oppressor.
We have too many come to confess
and wrongly, *it must be, must have been me*
or cried for no discernable reason
staring through starlight at a dark freedom.

Dreaming Again of You Last Night

You drove the car. We were going somewhere.
Weather was not a factor insofar
as all the roads were dry and bare. The tracks
seemed polished, silver in the big fat sun
and the conductor brought us frozen drinks
pastel and slushy just how you like them.
Smooth and cool. Lake George I think. No, Placid,
maybe on Saranac you drove the boat
with a posed élan, as if new to it.
Your hair was long and red again and flew
behind in the slipstream, wild as can be.
In the mirrors of your shades there was me
clutching my Lake Placid cap for dear life
and we were us again. You were my wife
our glorious lives restored to us there
in animations of our alive days
a little Chris-Craft speeding in sunlight.
Those eternal airplanes never crashing—
contrails stretching in a diamond-blue sky
it seems so true, the truth of us laughing.

Under the Thousand Gilded Domes

I

We read, or we had read to us beautiful,
awakening truths, Sappho to Eliot.
Rapturous outbursts were not unusual
in two ancient tongues—awe-struck, we cherished it,
first in our lineage gone away to school—
the first Catullus, the first Modern British.
This was our Exodus, from the rolling mill
and at less than the shop steward's liquor bill.

II

First ones to have it, first ones to squander it,
this is corruption, this is corruption's way.
Thus do our Puritans, free as they want it
chase Roger Williams from Massachusetts Bay,
take to weird shibboleths, *love it or leave it,*
veni vidi vici, y'all have a nice day.
Just do as I say, children, not as I do,
I'm free, white, and twenty-one, Daddy, and you?

III

If John Cameron Swayze would sell you a watch
or if Cronkite an inflated body count
it was Timex, it was the Army in doubt,
not them. Twenty-six minutes, or close—not this

our sun and moon of it, endless gibberish—
taunting the elderly with the End of Days.
Emigrants, *truthy* now, we made a strange choice,
we want lies of our own, in the loudest voice.

This Is to Thank You My Dear Past

I can't help it if I'm lucky.
— Bob Dylan

I had to be there to be here, I think.
I saw from great loneliness, illusion
but found the soft landing from every brink.
I saw from great happiness, illusion.
From elves in the cypress I drew no link
to illness or madness or confusion.
I majored in English for Heaven's sake
in the manner of Coleridge and Blake.

Oh you poor sad lot of students today
in the reign of commodification,
how you have trod trod trod for the big "A,"
reading those books on summer vacation—
for whom it is impossible to pay,
to *take* Herodotus in translation.
No sage, venerable antiquary,
joyous elves hiding in the library.

Two kinds of Seventeenth Century Lit,
your Cavalier, your Metaphysical,
every single day on fire with it
and every single moment lyrical,
teeming Victorian or Modern Brit—
just all of it towering wonderful.
Oh our fine children, so square and uptight,
for *privilege* mocking us, fair, true and bright.

A Letter to the Editor

They came to seem strangely obsessed
with a hermitic privacy, in a communal certainty
as to things rightly spoken, or rightly repressed
in the established wisdom of custom and courtesy.

All were protected. From a lover's too-lush, reminiscent ardor
or the bewildered longing of a former communicant's heart.
From crack-pots and flimflammers who each day try harder,
tooth from jaw, red from blue, to cleave them apart.

Thus did the elders in the name of civility,
in a hackneyed comity set forth these edicts
and all were agreed, free of a neighborly or a civic duty:
No sex spoken here, no religion, no politics.

The notice of liberation rang in their ears. From their lips,
weather reports. Images flashed, the thousand-year
storm of television news, the twenty-four-hour apocalypse
and no one said *boo,* such a thing not being proper there.

Cooped Up

They can beat you bad in behavioral.
Totally mean treatment—they skate from it.
When you are psychotic—try not to go.
They have had it with sick people, you know.
You could rip a doctor's eyeglasses off.
Crumble them up. Bare-handed, squash 'em to bits,
so bloody & all, you are in for some shit.
Sucker punches, low blows, kung fu, judo.
Restraining devices, kicks in the ribs—
the posse—pissed-off security—don't go.
Trickery and happy-talk, mom-like voices,
three days they tell you, but you never know.
Doped-up citizens, the thousand-yard stare
and Doctor Creepy has an extra pair.

Why He Speaks Freely of a Psychiatric History

No reason to hide it now, he'd say.
Maybe he's proud of it, just being alive.
Maybe he *is* a sensationalist.
All of those grim, sensational stories, hilarious, loving
or not. Hilarious, loving, false or true—

who among us really knows the difference?
He was her lover in the long-ago—
Anabelle believed—Agostino was too.
The toy of an ancient need, he wondered,
maybe it's true. Her daughter, the droll one said,

She has had a few. He was hurt (why not?)
by the nonagenarian's duplicitous fantasy.
At the end of her hospice, a last dream
for the worthy siren of an asylum.
Soon enough too for the whole, sad, fated crew.

What of the shaves and haircuts, of the socks
festooned with all manner of bird, cat or fish,
of what seemed a final embrace,
a family Christmas in the common room—
glassy-eyed Pop-Pop, all fallen apart,

those eccentric, aspirational gifts
at the nexus of sentiment and passion?
What to do with our history of lies
wherein ancestors died of contagion
or snakebite, not of an institution?

Five thousand years of it hidden away,
kept in the closets, swept under the rugs
until in a single generation,
from the madhouse to psychotropic drugs
some people got free—you, maybe, maybe me.

In the Season of Sleeping Late

It's as if they think we will not notice,
these platoons, these squadrons of physicians
in our triannual perfunctories.
Kicks at the tires, peeks under the hood.

We know why no more is necessary
at a certain age, or does very much good.
Our dwindling portion of ten thousand steps,
of heartbeat counts in the aerobic zone.

We know. And mostly answer honestly
those obtrusive, those odious questions.
Do you dine in company, or alone?
One whisky, is it, or two—and your goals,

your goals in the darkening good evening
there in the hidden-most season gazing
toward a hidden, inescapable fact—
out into the cold, the beautiful gloom?

Desire This Living Moment

Nothing is true anymore.
— a citizen

The age of professors is come and gone.
The age of evidence is come and gone.
Everything turns on desire, we knew it
all, all along.
To whom to say *thank you*, to whom
to say *good night*—our *Siri* or *Alexa*
as with leaden eyes we close the book again.
Whether to be perfunctory,
whether to be polite, to purchase
a thing or two before bed?
Our coming and going certainties—
then and now comingling, hurt
and want and having it and loss
to linger in the Great Suspension.
An empty glass a fire withering—then,
now, presence, absence—same thing.

When Each Important Thing Happens Elsewhere

And nothing seems to be before me here
all morning, all evening I remember.
All afternoon, well or poorly, I sleep
under a blanket of Bach or Mozart
courting new dreams of Elysian fields.

Neither in indifference nor defiance
nor even in the preference of my will—
it seems there is no better medicine.
In these cantata-laden dreams of mine
the weather is fair, the days beginning,

the unturned Earth warm in the rising sun
and we are born again and wise this time
and free of the old, meaningless bromides
so easily bent into purposes.
My children live next door—their children too

who make their little ruckus in the hall
to probe the last partita with their lilt—
the chorus of an endless baseball game,
notes from a schoolyard those ages ago
waking me now, just before dinnertime.

The Painted Desert

Where the stars do not so much pierce darkness
as let it be known. Time turns a tree into stones
pretty as glistening flowers, imperfect gems,
those geode bookends cut against a grain
and polished to a fare-thee-well. Ocherous
pastels and tawny—a yielding ground
so similar in its way to a fallen snow.
Into a loamy world you flop and dive
though you cannot make imprints of angels.
Where in a cold, stunning aridity
the earth will not stick to you.
Where you fall and rise-up, so easily,
so completely brush-off your coat,
go back to Winslow for another night
wondering which of those images signify.

Deprivation

I have no home.
If you have no home, the cold and the heat.

I have no clothing.
If you have no clothing, your blistering skin.

I have nothing to eat.
If you have no food, scorn is your stalker.
The last of the Christians hangs on the Cross.

I have no love.
If you have no love, love is calling you—
you cannot hear in this noise—listen harder.

I cannot remember.
If you cannot remember, I will tell you a story.
We will huddle together and make a new world.
Delighting the Gods and the Angels and Saints,
shocking the neighbors, ours is the better creation.

But they will accuse us of blasphemy.
In the usual way of blasphemers
they will accuse us of blasphemy.

I am alone.
If you are alone, examine your conscience.

I have no friend.
If you have no friend, I will be your friend.

ACKNOWLEDGMENTS

Journal of New Jersey Poets: ". . . Like an Old Fool"

Natural Bridge: "Log Cabin Nut Brown"

The CC Villager: "On the Threshing Floor," "As to Our Evening Gaze," "Dissonance, Retirement Village," "Crossing Second Avenue," "To Sit Here at Night Alone," "In the Season of Sleeping Late," "When Each Important Thing Happens Elsewhere"

The Stillwater Review: "Screen Time," "Is It Blasphemy," "To an Old Woman in a Wheelchair"

This Broken Shore: "Melodiam Desiderata"

U S 1 Worksheets: "In the Silence of Olsen's Pines and Oaks," "First Comes Desire"

Sincerest thanks to David Crews and Elaine Koplow for their work on the manuscript. To Judith Ann Christian for her years of close-reading and collaboration. To David Greenwood and Lois Kipnis and the editors and staff of the *CC Villager*, a private quarterly journal of arts and letters, for their kindness to my poems, and to the publisher Karunesh Kumar Agarwal for his friendship over now these four volumes and a dozen years. And of course, to Terry Ann Futcher, the inestimable paragon to whom this collection is dedicated.

meteor dense
it strains at the bud from all time
the iris next spring
suddenly purple

ABOUT THE AUTHOR

Chuck Tripi is a retired airline pilot and executive living in Pompton Plains, New Jersey, USA. With his late wife Barbara he was founding partner of the Paulinskill Poetry Project, a boutique press and community resource. His poetry appears widely in journals and other media, *Boston Review, California Quarterly, Louisiana Literature, Poet Lore,* and *Quiddity* among them. His collections include *Carlo and Sophia*, a Cyberwit bestseller (2013), *Killer Pavement Ahead* (Cyberwit, 2015), and *Wander Where They Will* (Cyberwit, 2022).